The Raz/Shumaker Prairie Schooner Book Prize in Poetry

EDITOR Kwame Dawes

"The poems are necessary and compressed, often couplets. Nothing here is excessive, except life. The poet is fully mature and brilliantly accomplished. The tragedy of immigration, and its necessity, are defined with precision and passion. Diseases are diagnosed by needle biopsy. Conditions have names as sonorous as Armenian. The poems look forward and backward, always led by language. They transfer states of mind into space travel. They ponder similarities between a dead tooth and a dead parent. And always they speak what we must hear. 'Self-pity can be poetry,' Bedikian notes. 'Show me one death that is a complete sentence.' I need this book and think you will, too." —HILDA RAZ, author of *Letter from a Place I've Never Been: New and Collected Poems, 1986–2020*

"Lory Bedikian has created a monument of rage in facing the march of calamities against a life. That list of constant misfortune begins with her family displacement from a homeland, the multiple poverties of a refugee existence, through each parent's loss. Each loss of an identity displaces the voice of the narrator, within time, between persons, even dismantling emotion. Is it the mother or daughter speaking; against each other, or in a rage of love for each other? Is it the caregiver or the patient who rages against the illness's damage to love? This kind of shapeshifting allows varieties of poetic form, all engaged in this consistently coherent polemic of rage. How deeply and broadly this rage can inform a life. *Jagadakeer: Apology to the Body*'s world will be very disconcerting—yet rewarding—to readers of this exquisitely composed work." —ED ROBERSON, winner of the PEN/Voelcker Award for Poetry and author of *To See the Earth Before the End of the World*

"Bedikian's poems speak to what becomes 'the ritual of tears,' of the long trip to America, 'the east coast's cold,' its 'stifled air of small apartments.' In this book she declares herself the daughter of a people who suffered and sang, worked and wept, speaking the language they remembered in. And so the daughter remembers for them, giving them a voice and us a smudged window through which to see the burning world. A consummate craftsperson, Bedikian writes lushly, with power and force, creating images we cannot unsee. Open this book and read her poem 'Before the Elegy, Speak to Her,' and see what I mean." —DORIANNE LAUX, author of *Only As the Day Is Long*

"Clear-eyed and beautiful, the poems in Lory Bedikian's *Jagadakeer: Apology to the Body* navigate a generational inheritance of trauma and anger with unflinching awareness, tenderness, and sharp-edged humor. I encourage you to read this collection from front to back, as the opening sections lay the foundation for a tremendous exploration of the interior of a life. There is so much hard-earned wisdom throughout, with a speaker that tells us 'laughter is not happiness // after all, but the machinery of the body undoing anger,' and 'Don't love // what I say because you think you should. Love / what you hear because it makes you // question everything.' I love what this book has to say and 'I want everyone to stand up to choir it out. Even the dead.'" —BRIAN TURNER, author of *Here, Bullet* and *The Goodbye World Poems*

Jagadakeer: Apology to the Body

Lory Bedikian

University of Nebraska Press / Lincoln

Acknowledgments for the use of copyrighted material appear on
pages 99–100, which constitute an extension of the copyright page.

The University of Nebraska Press is part of a land-grant institution
with campuses and programs on the past, present, and future
homelands of the Pawnee, Ponca, Otoe-Missouria, Omaha, Dakota,
Lakota, Kaw, Cheyenne, and Arapaho Peoples, as well as those
of the relocated Ho-Chunk, Sac and Fox, and Iowa Peoples.

Library of Congress Cataloging-in-Publication Data
Names: Bedikian, Lory, author.
Title: Jagadakeer: apology to the body / Lory Bedikian.
Description: Lincoln: University of Nebraska Press, 2024. | Series:
The Raz/Shumaker Prairie Schooner book prize in poetry
Identifiers: LCCN 2024002396
ISBN 9781496240125 (paperback)
ISBN 9781496241276 (epub)
ISBN 9781496241283 (pdf)
Subjects: BISAC: POETRY / American / General | LCGFT: Poetry.
Classification: LCC PS3602.E342 J34 2024 |
DDC 811/.6--dc23/eng/20240119
LC record available at https://lccn.loc.gov/2024002396

Designed and set in Garamond by L. Welch.

In memory of
  Vahan Bedikian, 1931–2018,
  and Zevart Bedikian, 1937–2020

even with dry sticks I can't get started
even with thorns.

—Adrienne Rich, "The Phenomenology of Anger"

CONTENTS

Yehs [means *I* in Armenian]

In Lieu of an Epilogue

Jagadakeer: In Remission

Jagadakeer: Apology to the Body

Ode to Their Leaving

As if the sky which darkened on that monumental day, the day Lebanon
　　would be left behind for you both, the day all relations, kin,
　　　　unshaven onlookers

grit their teeth or the *kyughatsees*, village women began the ritual of tears
　　handkerchiefs tied to the trees, the sheep slaughtered for the last feast,

as if the flight above the Atlantic and all the cirrus clouds bowing to the course,
　　the passport the husband opens and closes over and over again

knowing he may lose them all, to another set of civil unrests, another war
　　calculated like the backgammon board too large and burdensome to
　　　　bring along,

as if the teeth of the east coast's cold, the stifled air of the small apartments
　　the lies that led to the losing of jobs they said would replenish

the spent money, as if all of this was not enough of a cauldron, a wingless griffin,
　　the husband dies first, a year later the wife dies, and these two called

father, *mother* in one's eeriest and quietest sleep, not birth-like or dream-like,
　　but the time of post-midnight hallucinatory lullabies and afterthoughts.

Why do you not say who you are? Say it. Say *daughter*. Daughter holding genetics
　　of immigrant ink stains, holding the small histories of their breakfast
　　　　blabbering.

And so what did you know of their demise? Father scanned the news of the world,
　　knew the guilt of countries and mustached biographies, while he never

spoke of his ills. The spine fractured, the valves road blocked, the vocal cords
　　bombed. If anger was his food, then food was his poison. The bites didn't

matter, the morsels mother fed him mocked even the smallest capillaries.
  And mother

        did you tell him what was coming or did you decide to follow?
          Is it a daughter's

greatest sin to ask? But look how quiet I am. I watch the world cry itself to sleep.
        I pinch the spices into their bowls as you did the day you were married,

          as you did on the unbelievable days you died.

Hiereeg [means *father* in Armenian]

Meditation on Fractured Vertebrae

Praise the backbone, praise the lumbar curve,
      trust the spine that once held you up behind

the pulpit, that altar of polished oak, black bible in hand,
      trust the palm raised toward the stained-glass dove.

Father, open your ears to the congregation calling *Bahdveli*,
      pastor, come and bless us this broken day,

damn it, hear the choir singing their guttural Armenian
      raising up *praise God from whom all blessings flow*.

When you bend that way you are headed straight for the ground.
      Stand straight as the columns of Baalbek,

those stone exclamations that held the Lebanese sky, legs
      of ruined gods rooted, planted into the parched earth,

while we spoke of lost classmates and empires. Black gown
      in the closet. Kaleidoscope stole in its petrified spiral.

Beg, baba, plead, baba, say take me back to my *Halebtsi*-girl
      her cat glasses leaning off Aleppo's balcony,

rue of dust that will never leave the lung alone,
      wife who now wipes your forehead with thunder and psalms

while the dreams come, young again, a bowl of roasted quail
      presented after the first sermon, pushed the congregation

to crowded streets, to the confetti of pistachio shells, innocent
      ammunition of the boys who hid from the sweat-drenched pews.

Hard to believe blessings flow, when you've come so far
      from orphaned tenements. The nurses hoist you

in a wheelchair, feed you food coarse as gravel. Hard
    to believe so many relatives have gone

from the earth, through the mouth of war, by the claws
    of illness. Unfair. We're so unfair to say

lay hands on each bone, transform them into stalactites,
    stalagmites of Jeita Grotto, that white chamber,

those limestone caves you took her to, so far from Beirut,
    you thought you'd reached the sun,

she thought you'd reached heaven at last, her headband,
    your argyle bowtie, away from the tenor

voices crowding the chorus, away from mosquito
    nets of seminary, calligrapher's ink on the splintered sill,

far from the Syrian pine that spied the window.
    I call you *baba* again. You hear me now and then.

I mumble *ahmen*. The land of amber, turquoise, remains
    in the candy wrappers of mother's purse. This *ahmen*

to heal it all, *ahmen* for where you grew in the acreage of kings,
    where winds mussed your coiled hair, now in hospital beds

of the new world. You're almost gone. The road to Aleppo rises,
    mother's headband in the first pew, hymnals close,

heads bow down, eyes lower when your devotional has begun,
    everyone at the call of benediction, you looking straight ahead.

Father dreams of Gibran

They are turning cups of coffee over
to tell each other's fortunes. Khalil says

the sky is growing its beard, the darkness
an inevitable departure. My father turns over

pistachio shells to make small mounds
on the table, their mahogany becomes a desert.

Say they are brothers, for in this moment they are.
Khalil tells him there is no other way of being.

Father holds his face in his palms, distraught
as if the birds had brought bad news again.

Lebanon, 1932, Khalil has not died
but instead intoxicates himself with anise,

slow poems on the tongue, dissolving.
Say things will improve, but they won't.

Buildings will fall, bodies will clutter
dirt roads, children will believe in nothing.

Decades later an orphanage the size
of a bird's nest will open itself to fissures

of light, names of parents forgotten.
If anyone could reassure my father

that another road will open ahead of them
it was Khalil, his hands stained crimson,

kaleidoscope pieces of oil paint on his coat.
Lebanon, 1932, father born the year before,

nevertheless, at this roadside café they sit solid
as cave rocks, debating on their next move

in backgammon. Father asks him
if he is afraid of death. Khalil laughs.

Father asks him if he and his wife
will make it to the new world. Questions

litter the night like the gutter rats,
the mosquitos who bite and thrive.

No wonder it takes so long for my father
to wake. We wait by his bedside, impatient

for a word or open eye. His stroke
another step closer to closing his world,

his tracheotomy a fiddle in the fire.
No wonder no one can nudge him

to consciousness. Why would a man
want to come back to our moment,

so far from his newfound brother,
who meets him every day to discuss

the stubborn cedar trees, the impossible
bond of the sparrow and the bulbul

in the midst of shrapnel and ouzo
despite the oncoming decades

as unpredictable as the letters
they don't dare to open and read.

Theorizing Vahan's Departure

But what if the black hole is home,
what if where he lives now multiplies

song. I'm imagining that sand
doesn't burn even in the brightest hours,

the zenith can be viewed without damage.
Mother, let's not fear entrances and exits.

Instead, shred the photo album, make space
for his new childhood, which is everywhere

at once, resembling the windblown shore
they buried his brothers upon, Lebanon

galactic because it's all he knew, cedars
their own type of kin, lined on roads that

know no differences of seeds, bullets, coins.
Everyone back from diaspora they never asked for.

Maybe the black hole of the sky, the light
years of the mind are the only way

to be swallowed up, released, transferred
into a constellation summoned, the sun

unnecessary, the zodiac, its outstretched words
finally giving us, in starlight, omens, signs.

Mother, maybe our lesions are gold.

Psychosomatic disorder

A brother-in-law passes away
  he begins to lose things he once had,
   stride of his leg, sure step of foot,
repeat trills of his aged voice box.
   Next brother-in-law dies, he decides
    he can't stand anymore. He can't
stand more. Doctors yawn, specialists
  shrug shoulders. All that's put beside
   him turns reverse-placebo. The cure
resides in working backward, so we do.
   Letters from Lebanon came monthly, onion
    paper, smeared ink, his head began
low-pitched hits. Further back finds
  news his brethren have joined
   others somewhere in Cygnus
while his suburban home turns
  trenches, his eyes into artillery.
   His cousin in her egg-shelled
dementia screams his name, the two once children
  who left their homes when the tall
   army men came, said leave. Both now,
in different beds, feel the ghost boat
  moving, the heave-ho of the oars.
   Passed down and further down
everyone's wearing the clothes
  of the father, garbs of the mother.
   To save ourselves some of us sew stationery
to torn fabric of hand-me-downs,
  fly the horrendous quilt
   high upon a supernatural mast.

PART 2

Say what you want about
a gang of genes on chromosome six.

I'll tell you where it really started.
In Lebanon, of all places, they ask

if you'd like your aura read.
They say she's an expert.

Reads *something's wrong*.
Something in the head area.

Stuck on *oh my aura*,
my poor aura. Little did you know

she left quick, had a beer, while
you developed symptoms, scars.

After seeing the aftermath of war
you vomit while the Mediterranean glows.

As serious as bison, as charming
as a wombat, the man in Armenia

who beats his wife says you will
never marry because you're sitting

at the corner of the table, because
you drank the last drop of wine.

You contemplate his foresight, he offers
no antidote, opens a chestnut with his teeth.

Neurotic variation: you refuse a handsome boy's
advance at the opera. You sing *woe is me*.

The search for the beginning is endless,
jokes rebound. Immune system

took a back seat to your bundled nerves.
No one laughs in the mirrored medicine chest.

You contemplate grandmother's burning feet,
father's skull of pain, mother's hysteric

laugh married to a cry, brothers who
arm wrestle to win the next diagnosis,

sure you suffer from a slight case
of everything as you refuse to buy items

in twos, because what's the point.
It will all be over soon enough.

Chaparral

Each day is the day you might die.
We become accustomed to the arrival of news

that slips in and out of drama, routine.
You go everywhere we would never want to.

Your wife becomes the one who sits, stands,
signs paperwork she does not bother to read.

In the ICU the nurse's hand becomes your mother's.
It's 1931, the dust thickens on the sill, the door closes

with burlap and yarn. Your father has been awake
for hours before Alexandretta opens its eyes

to the broken orchards tended for years,
to pick and crate fruit, his wagon a makeshift

market. As you dream this, as you bring back
the Mediterranean shore your brothers bartered

on, Bagras Castle empty in the distance,
as your wife watches beeping screens,

an IV drips, indifferent, casual drops,
and I go back to a day away from all our doom.

Along the chaparral-covered slopes
of the San Gabriel Mountains before

the sage scrub, two steep gradients, two ravines
span the foothills and open up to a steady

sturdy man who climbs slowly upward,
his walking stick held like a line of latitude,

a slight exhaustion accompanies him
each day as I see him arrive to the trail,

punctual, stern as the men he came from, wiping
his forehead from the warm-up. When he reaches

his maximum point, he stops, turns.
I can never tell if he will stop breathing,

his chest erratic, untamable. But each day,
the same. He starts to speak, to himself, to no one.

The sky cracked, stunning. As if the big-cone spruce
woodland is his wife, long gone, he grumbles, grips

the stick until his knuckles turn yellow-white,
covers his eyes from the glare.

Somewhere nearby, a famous barn where a family
of winegrowers once lived. In 1933 a massive fire

burned the hillsides he stands on. The family
must have rebuilt, recovered, because the barn

remains at the vista point, stoic. Father, you were
overseas then, growing, gnawing on your fingers.

Your father sold a few crates, traded goods
not knowing what the news would be at dusk,

not knowing how long they would call it home.
The hospital is quiet tonight, like the chaparral-

covered hills. The man who walks alone
opens his bottle of wine and pours.

If only he had written his refugee song

If we broke the cliché in half and home
was not where the heart was but instead
where your body intended to remain,

that machine of pulse and memory,
skin its largest organ, the intricate map
of your life in sunspots, a chosen few

that began on farmland in Lebanon,
some that formed during walks along
the lost apricot orchards of Cupertino,

then perhaps you should have trusted
that broken chassis of yours, trusted all
angles of it and moved it across floors,

shuffle until you began to walk again.
How quiet the house became when you
refused to sing. I entered thinking

I'd find attempts, but there you sat in silence.
Any tent is paradise for the one who
has lost everything. The flap of its mouth

a makeshift threshold. The canvas walls
boundaries of light. I told you to forget
treachery, but your bifocals, skillfully

useless, came on and off to read the news,
to remind you of what had once been home
to you, to kin. I told you to tuck

displacement in the wicker basket,
but you had faith in nothing, except
in the failing of the world. We hoped

your limbs would burn like red dwarfs,
your mind would forget about highlands
and forgive the half-wits on the pages,

but you rusted in place, your mind drove
the road of the body to pieces, your hands
grasping at nothing but the splintered air.

WHEN YOU ARE WRITING
YOUR FATHER'S HEADSTONE

You don't want to believe that this is his forever,

That this is the way he leaves his mark in the world.

Yet, you think of all the adjectives, you remember the ring

From Lebanon, inscription *omnia vincit amor*,
Worn daily until the fingers gave out.

If we question if love really conquers all,
How do we get the headstone up?

A Caravaggio would be stylish,
But anti-who-he-was,

Overly dedicated to us, to the mind's cavernous lies.

The sun who is a sun of a
Sun of a sun of a sun of a sun.

[Muriel, I can't say a thing.]

If heaven is nothing but forgiveness,
then can I say what I want?

If ghosts still have feelings,
then I better watch what I say.

The Tooth is Dead

When you hear it, you don't expect to stay so still
    as if

it wasn't the tooth itself, but that someone, not something
    was gone,

not obliterated or demolished, but lifelessness had won
    yet again;

you don't expect that word to be used for a molar,
    a larger

part of the mouth's structure, so much use it's given
    over time

pulverizing animal and vegetable both. They didn't even use
    that word

when your father died, instead they told your brother
    expired

like a driver's license, a parking meter, machines maybe
    but not

your father. *Expired* is not good enough to say what's done
    when he

is done, passed, passed away, no, nothing is adequate
    sound-wise

so *dead* must have been coined for its monosyllabic
    mean, quick

consonant *d*-sound to consonant *d*-sound, we can't even
    say it

quick enough to be done with it because who would want
      a word

that lasts so long, an eon to express such a concept.
      Even in

Armenian we say *mehrav*, which means he/she/it died
      almost

beautiful, not too long, softer than *dead*, first using closed lips
      m—

the latter brings the top teeth to the bottom lip as if biting
      the lip

the act of disbelief. Did someone think of that? That the
      body

should say with the mouth, the word through the act of the mouth
      should

express what death means? Even saying they died, *mehran*,
      even that

sounds like a lovely name of one you met long ago and could
      never

forget, a night where you kept tripping on everything while
      laughing

through sips of cognac. What was this tooth to you anyway,
      this losing

a part of yourself for good almost seems like an insult.
      You recall

those sculptures, gorgeous, Rodin in rain, real and boundless
an ear

chipped off from an earthquake, how the ivy twists against the torso
while you

stare at its imperfections. The sculpture never dies. Even if destroyed.
And your tooth?

And your father? There are moments flung across the galaxies
that have

their importance rooted in the empty spaces they leave.
No sounds

good enough to tell you that it's over, the tooth, the mouth
the word.

Miereeg [means *mother* in Armenian]

Before the Elegy, Speak to Her

Zevart, before you decide to go

anywhere, let me construct a ship of books,

sailable & plenty, free of disease & car rides,

a ship anchored to everything & nothing,

Zevart of my birth, a name I will not

simplify for them. Let them say it.

Zevart. Zevart of rose petal jam & calluses,

your mother, a desert walk, her mother

hovering above sheep's brain stew,

Zevart. Zevart. All I have left

of my first blurred sight. All that's

left of my own name, its song—

leave now & I won't find the impossible

argument of daybreak. Depart if you want,

but the phone will keep ringing.

Voice of Zevart. Body of Zevart.

Bathing Zevart. The weight of your body

on my arm, as if holding a country.

May you never read this, never learn

what I've done. A tradition never yours

this scrawled before it should be, your name

a drum, the only part I'll borrow, and so,

Zevart. The rest can stay in their glass

cases. Remember how our folktales began?

Gar oo chee gar. Once there was & was not

a life we knew full of produce & price

tags, tell me again before you go there,

how you & one brother took James Dean

to be a god. Aleppo tired of you.

Your mother never done in the kitchen.

What is it now that I'm doing?

Did I actually think this would preserve you?

How can I close this, when a train could take you

through a tunnel, a bag of dates & walnuts

on your lap, sudden darkness while you chew,

snickering at what you were never taught.

What did I promise? Oh, yes. This.

Zevart. Zevart. Zevart.

Fragments of Melancholy from
Those Rooms, Those Rooms

You say

you don't

want to die.

It is the first time

you have said

the word *funeral*.

It is then

that I want

your body

to turn

into

a turquoise sculpture

some sort of god

museum-material

the type of deity

where a passerby utters

how beautiful

but terrifying.

Broccoli

Now that the damage has been done
with all your belongings boxed,

labeled, the lie of someday reopening,
father's suits, those little empty men,

your lifetime of jewelry fingerless,
your eyes shrinking into a dark starlight;

now that you've lost it all, dependence
left on the body, lungs full, bitterness, mold,

the structure falters with each slippered
step, how is it that I have the audacity

to bring you broccoli, something you say
you never ate in *Hahleb*, so you don't

have a taste for it, that small green tree
barely steamed, barely a tree, more like small

stubbornness in the form of vegetable,
its stalk of vitamin and two thousand years,

its powers something you almost despise
until I tell you it will help. Help. Help you

never received enough of when he left
to join the sick of the world, those who wed

hospital beds, wilt so well it's almost evil,
a refrain that does not stop repeating,

help you should have seen in the shape
of a new home, instead of wild boars and rifles.

Just look, I say, the toasted sesame oil is divine,
good, will make it edible, the soy sauce made

of beans that they haven't cloned, all of it
confettied with peanuts, almond slivers;

oh mother, I can't save you. Even momentarily,
I can't send you back to the humid rooftops

of Aleppo, where the stories have no middle or end,
just the preface of that's what we did, that's

where we slept when the nights sweltered.
You've kept your stories from me. Hid

even the footnotes. Now I fabricate my own.
Tell them though it won't get us what we need,

cash of the dented world, easy life, money I've cursed,
wealth that should have been shared, even though

that golden ticket is trash now. Money won't save
even them when it's time. Bank accounts of smoke.

Sometimes we laugh. We recall how many idiots,
aboushnehr we've known. And yet we've survived.

In my imagination I'm building you a cottage,
though I almost hated you once, said what kind

of woman treats her daughter like that. Broccoli
is sympathy. It says that despite all the poison

preordained, consume me. Bite this green belief,
better than a leaf of lettuce, better than bread,

grind it between the teeth that should have bitten
hands of those who served it to you, the nerve

to want to make things better; although the house
is gone, your husband has joined your dark starlight,

you walk the halls thinking I don't want this
cane, this is not the way I wanted to go.

The pharmaceutical that killed my mother

wept by her bedside.

I asked it who it was and it replied

I was meant to prevent one thing,

but I caused another. How it wept, as if it had known her.

Its noise became so large

that the halls, the nurses' station oscillated

and while my mother wrung what was left

of her hands, in her dream, the oxygen machine

began to speak. It said words we hadn't

heard since her first flight to the new world:

Hahsahnk? Have we arrived? I tell

the drug it's lucky the world is in mourning

or you'd see my revenge.

I do not tell my mother something

smaller than her open eye left

an invasion in her lungs. I do not mention

that suddenly the sky is an epidemic,

that the cryptic, small print won.

Syllabics for My Mother

Your moan, the music of the old country,
your breathing evil in its staccato

taunt. How father haunts the eucalyptus
of the fourth-floor window. Miraculous

the heart continues though the rest shuts down,
the body contemplating afterlife

and its many-splendored topographies.
Die if you must. Leave if you really can't

hold conversations, shred historic maps,
pray with anger, gasp, kneel horizontal,

whatever works, look, it's not that different
than what you imagined and all is free.

On the wipe-off board the word *companion*
to alert the staff this woman wants friends,

someone to hear her moan incessantly.
Yes, of course. More than the oxygen tank,

the antibiotics filling her lungs,
she needs just one, her husband's surrogate,

because his singing voice, his ring, his clothes
gone in a suitcase. Someone surely knew

the lonely accelerate their exit
when there's no one to hear them. To be heard.

Is that it? The moaning sound only when
someone's there, the nurse reports. No wonder

you keep telling me to leave, soon after
I arrive. It's not enough to see if

I see your open eyes. You want me to
hear your cry. I shush you and you oblige.

Zevart, Ode to Joy

The name Zevart in the Armenian language means happy or joyous

Zevart, Ode to Joy: Introduction to Her Demise

When you lose a mother you lose the source. When you lose an Armenian
  mother you lose a seed far from its fruit.

Maybe there isn't anything more than what you remember at the end.

Where does the poison of a family come from? From the unsaid wish or
  the bottom of the well?

Antidotes barely in mushrooms and the memory of Doris Day.

Who feeds the sick arsenic for a year?

There are men who use funerals as doormats.

And so it should be said that she who loses her mother has the right to lose her
  bitterness as well. And she who loses her mother, while always respecting her
  memory, does not owe it to the soul of the departed to suddenly befriend the
  kin. Let the kin eat cake.

I say tell me what you remember. Tell me about Aleppo. She says
  "ask your aunt. You are all exhausting me."

An old man in a wheelchair has a backgammon board on his lap, which looks
  older than him. I say "how beautiful." He says "I don't know."

A woman in the hallway is screaming and hitting anyone who comes near her.

I cut all of my mom's nails. She tells me I did a fantastic job.

God give me strength.
God give me strength.

When they say her lungs
have only a thimble of space
left for oxygen,
it has taken over,
I become anxiety, I run.
Reverend Emma says
breathe for her. Breathe
in her direction.

Zevart, Ode to Joy: Her Only Memoir

I know nothing about my father.

~

My father had bought a sheep.

We'd wake up in the mornings, go to a small hill. We'd take our breakfast with
us, we'd sit and eat. We would watch the sheep graze.

I'll never forget that.

Something different.

Ajourtallah to *Nor Kyoogh*—people came and went. *Nor Kyoogh* was
where the Armenian churches were.

Of course the sheep would later become food.

~

My friend Hasmig was on the other side of town. She was my friend during
high school.

~

At home, with my grandmother and mother, we would hand-wash laundry
in a tub, we would pull water up from the well. The bucket. The rope.

~

In the corner of the yard my father had built an area to press grapes. He'd tell
us come on, wash your feet and press. We'd use the juice for *bahstukh*.

~

There were no planes to go to America from Syria so we went to Lebanon.
Everyone came to say goodbye.

~

My brother told me high school is enough for you, enough for a woman.
You don't need college.

~

I taught kindergarten for a year. That's where I met your father—he was the
minister of the school and a teacher and fell in love with me.

At recess he'd speak to me.

~

Supposedly, he saw a dream that he brought my family a bowl of fruit.
That's what he told me.

~

I'm walking a long distance on the snow from our house to school.
Elementary-school age. And with every few steps I see a coin on the snow.
It was so exciting. I'll never forget this. I picked up each one. There must
have been a hole in some fool's pocket.

~

Desert countries: the summer's so hot, the winter's terribly cold.

~

When it was the first snow of winter, we'd take a cupful, put some sort of syrup on it and eat it. Actually, my grandmother and her friend would want it more than we would and they would send us out. They would send us out and we'd get it for them. They loved it. We ate some too.

~

When I took you there, do you remember? You remember, right? You remember Aleppo? You lowered a basket from the second-story window to the man selling goods, baked goods, *kekhgeh*. You were only two. Always the money in the basket first. He would take the money and you pulled up the food. You loved that.

~

[singing] *karoun karoun karoun eh, seeroon, seeroon, seeroon eh, eht koo sev sev atchkerov, yar jahn eendzee eyeroom ehs.*

You'd dance with the neighbor's girl.

~

Stepan diedie loved music from America—he'd go to American movies playing at *Cinema Sooria*.

~

We lived in a two-bedroom home. One bedroom was for my father, mother, for me and for Maral.

The other bedroom was where my brothers slept. My father's mother, Ferideh, slept in that room too.

~

There's something else. I don't know if it's important. I don't know if you want to hear it.

Movses diedie had a coffee shop in Aleppo College. He rented it, where students ate, had coffee. So my father and mother used to make homemade mortadella and hummos. My mother, early in the morning, would take the bus and go all the way to Aleppo College to deliver those things. There was a young man, my classmate. My mother would spread hummos in pita bread and give it to him to eat. He was poor.

[On television, an Armenian program, *yes kez keech em seerel, too eem myreeg.* Sung by a woman in a blue gown, roughly meaning *I don't love you enough, mother.*]

~

Zevart, Ode to Joy: Epilogue

She no longer wants to color what is left of her hair or wear lipstick. I say "you have visitors, don't you want to?" She says "it's just all of you." I say "it was all of us before." She says, "It's different now. I'm sick."

"My arms. Why are they so tired? What do my arms have to do with anything?"

Fragment

Your coffin, that sad box.

            But which one of you

is in this one. *Eenie meenie minie . . .*

            One dies & then the other

shortcuts, clips eternity

            into a paper snowflake.

I don't trust the leftovers

            [Muriel, I'm afraid]. I know

of pickpocketed, recounted stars

            above your deathbeds.

I understand science, but

            where did you go?

Sestina, as my mother cooks

I tell her it's a problem of the nerve.
She doesn't look up but eases a scar
on each small olive, making room
for the marinade to soak in. Not one eye
blinks as she does this. Like before, I'm pretty
sure that this is my cue to leave.

But I think back, when she had to leave
Aleppo with my father, each goodbye plucking a nerve,
hitting notes against her chest—quite pretty
for a plainly dressed Protestant. Like a scar
they mark the bible with this date. One eye
on the future, they fly and find a one-room

apartment in New York. Now, my mother acts as if this room
holds only her. She mumbles there's nothing wrong, just leave
the past alone and you'll be fine. I lunge my twitching eye
toward her. But she doesn't have the nerve
to look. I wonder how she handles the brush of scar
below her abdomen, where I entered the world, pretty

different than most. She asks me to put on something pretty
for once. The L.A. noon heat rises. I pace the room
thinking of how to tell this woman of the scar
tissue the doctor found; how I tried to leave
the office smiling, grateful it wasn't worse, just a nerve
disorder, its radar placed in the sphere of an eye.

After so many years, she still gives me the eye
over. What I say next is anything but pretty:
Has she ever thought each cell, each nerve
of my body is conspiring in rebellion to the room

we've always held between us? She says she must leave
for work, she's late. My fingers shake. I say another scar

will form from this—like each scar
you brought across the Atlantic. I feel as small as the eye
of a needle. A cutting board, an empty sink is what we leave
behind us. She walks ahead, down the hall. I stop. Pretty
soon she'll reappear. In this house I have no room
left, so I grab my keys, knowing it's enough that I've struck this nerve.

This is how she survives, making sure to leave the house looking pretty.
Not one scar visible to the eye. She doesn't question this world, how it has
the nerve to move us from room to room, so far from where we started.

Another word for bitterness is ache

If you ask the daughter what started it all, she most probably
won't blame the metronome at the top of the piano.

Her mother always wanted to play the piano
            and since she never learned, then the daughter had to

      fill that void. No matter that the daughter, (the *her* now)
wanted a Fender instead of a generic version of a Wurlitzer

up against a space worse than Gilman's yellow wallpaper,
            —something she would later read, recognize, how if men

      tell women what's wrong with them then more than hell
has broken loose, more than the underworld—wanted

to strum chords, break scales, use a fret to tame the wild
            of her own hair. The metronome was not the problem.

      It was a gift from her aunt. The metronome was owned,
unlike the no-name piano that was rented until this

daughter could learn how to play Fur Elise right.
            It may be important to mention here that the neighbors

      had a piano and a daughter and piano lessons lined up,
but the piano was their own and the father was a machinist.

The *her* filling the void had a father who could recount
            the history of Mesopotamia while singing Nessun Dorma,

      but worked as a salesman, the type with a name tag.
If this family created its own archetype of the mother figure

it would be a female deity with great shoes, a Syrian passport
            and one who has mastered the art of rationalizing anything.

But what started it all could never be figured out because
no one ever learned to play the piano or the guitar,

and the mother, gone now, only reminds the daughter
        that familial stories are mythology with name tags.

    In this story, the daughter never truly learns to play
any instrument and instead considers that mahogany

may actually be the greatest word ever invented, alongside
        the greatest flower, the ranunculus, because this flower

    is honest, it wilts sooner than later, the sphere of its bloom
so impossible to unravel and barely scented, no thorn in sight.

Take a story like this, without plot, beginning or end
        insert the music the piano could have played and one can hear

    a bruised E major, a sullen D minor and the tearing in half
of borrowed sheet music, of the newest unpaid bills.

Yehs [means *I* in Armenian]

Apology to the Body

Sorry for mercury strewn in veins of fish,
for traces of carbon monoxide loose in the air,
for radiation that circles and enters the aura.

Sorry for deliberate puffs and sips
late in the night, for an empty stomach
burning with coffee grounds,

for words of magma, thoughts rough as tufa
scratching the indivisible cells, fragile nerves,
divisions of labor and function,

for scraping skin until it bled, garnet
scars in constellation form, for chemicals
bathing in a pool of genetics, under viral stars.

I'm looking to cleanse regret. I want to give
you a balm for lesions, give you evening
primrose, milk thistle, turmeric, borage,

feet moving toward a language
of trees, hands deciphering sediment, steady
rhythm back in the pulse, the breathing you knew

before you were born. Believe me that we began
together and I will mend each sheath of myelin,
reverse the dark that grows behind my eyes.

Looking at the MRI Six Years Later

I can't seem to get it right,
how to name the patterns

of what I've become. Ashen leaves
against a charcoal branch, or dead

blotches of smoke. I want to say
shapes like coral reefs float in film,

but then I see water stains left
on a wooden table. The cerebrum

dims, half-moons in cerebellum
prick orbs in medulla oblongata.

I can't seem to trace
how it all started, these wild

mushrooms growing inside of me,
these decayed walnuts in dark shells.

And then I see what it is.
I've been stricken with *altocumulus*. Almost

a decade, I've been carrying rain clouds
in the skull. Drenched rags hover above,

lightning and thunder beat a wild drum,
but no downpour comes.

Year after year the spotted sky grows
darker, it waits for gray lesions

to start a storm.

Beloved Denial

Each morning can be a miracle or the same lie
you've been telling yourself for a decade and a half

that no matter what flaw may show itself
through magnetic fields, through radio waves,

the epitome of good health walks in your shoes.
You can tell yourself this as you told yourself

that you were not clawing at your skin,
scraping blemished olive epidermis,

your inheritance of a landlocked map.
Development became arrested through

hits of arms, screams into keyholes.
Mother said show skin. Father said no boys.

You were taught to press vespers into
yourself, but the nerves couldn't endure

immune's abusive ways. You can enter black
holes of genetics and still manage to return.

You can claim optic neuritis is the bipolar
disorder of the camphor trees who believe

they are made of cellophane—no, rugs.
After all, you weren't born to be scarred.

You don't mind lying to yourself about this.
Honest about everything else, really. Except

how you haven't kissed fear on his mouth,
wicked, secret boyfriend who wants you to

lie after hours, hush-hush love, complain
of neurological backdoors, him pressing

into all of your fire-breathing refusals,
as if you could catch something from his lips,

something contagious, almost permanent.

Ode to Illness: rant in the form of monologue

I don't believe in you.

You're just a beekeeper working
overtime, buzz in the shoulder, buzz

in the stomach, the lungs. Form a planetary
mishap and we've spelled your name again.

Barking dog of our bodies, sculptor of disorder.
Hey. Listen. We want devotion, not a eulogy.

Theopathy can be a fortress if used
as a field guide. Put the hands together in prayer

and one can say not every ailment follows disaster,
not every lab result begs for mercy. Some of it

genetic, sure, but some of it remains just a bed of coals.
Throw an axle in the organized alphabet and what

ends up is certainly gibberish. Forget a future obituary,
forget the skull and crossbones, irritable cells

under the machines, the magnification. Behold
what we've hidden and you scan and decipher

the igneous rock of our chassis. Behold years,
decades, weariness in muscles, iceberg veins

that defend themselves from puncture saying
I am mouthless.

Family says Dehdeh died

of malaria. Syria. The early 1900s. There was a time
the documents could have been found, but leave it

to bombs to erase the records of everything.
Aren't you something like a bomb, a grenade?

Aren't you the reason we fear gas to flame?
That's like you, isn't it—a geologist who has no

insomnia but dreams of planets as well as earth.
I don't believe in your gauze, miles of destruction,

I don't believe in being exiled from health
just because you think every moment is a universe.

Politician. Tainted relative. Your integrity is the disposed
syringe. Right in the ear, right in the damn ear you whisper:

there are healing properties particularly in nothing special. Sold.
Because of you, it's acceptable to talk about an uncle's kidneys.

OK to discuss an upheld son's woes. But not the daughter.
Shush her up. *Amote eh*: It's shameful. They don't need

to know.

Amote eh, Amote eh.

No talk about daughter, female, sister. Change the subject.
No chat about ruined-she. Erase her diagnosis of scars

on the brain, stains on the spine, typos on the mind,
lesions, multiplied, many reasons behind each one.

There was once a time it was easy to speak of you.
You entered, whittled, ate, ravaged, then left. Usually

your exit included the body's departure, we gave you
more than you needed in order to make sense of you.

Hypocrite. Holding out the examination gown
in your long arms, reminding us that you don't have

to stay

                unless we argue and insist.

Hypochondria

If only you had been that flower
the family would call out with fervor
ee-aa ending your name, a universal sound
so many enamored with, first the teeth showing
then the mouth ready for examination.
But you're no plant, animal, vegetable
nothing to put our aging hands on.
Just once again a cerebral impasse.
Delusion, listen. You've got to find
another place to pitch that tent.
The belief is still out there that civil unrest
began by planting disease-carrying parasites
in the desired nutmeat of walnuts.
No one's getting better. One fears the worst.
The other fears everyone they see and don't.
Never mind real infections, fabricated
fibromyalgia. Attractive as hell,
none of them admit falling for you.
Centennial of grandfather's medical journal
open to the page he was on when he fell
asleep for good. Genealogy creeps up
on us as we beseech all we know
for cures we have never even heard of.

Needle Biopsy

We watch what we think is hesitance
        as its long legs enter the stream's edge

after a few moments we call forever,
        and even then, the movement

deliberate, slow, what fear might look like.
        Someone close by guesses *crane*,

someone else jokes *albatross*,
        while it continues its measured pantomime.

We wait as if we understand, our eyes
        on the blue-gray body, its plumage

a motionless splendor high above
        the soon-to-be-caught pathetic prey.

Amazed at how it has adapted to this life:
        creek bed at its disposal, nearby lake

dotted by open mouths of camellias.
        Days before we had seen this great blue heron,

I, too, entered a procedure, cautious,
        believing the day could continue

unscathed despite protocols, alterations.
        To adapt is survival. So I sign paperwork,

fasten ties of an examination gown, pace
        words so as not to say too much at once.

As I think this, with no falter of step or target,
        the majestic bird strikes the water, its neck

a frog's tongue, its bill a sharp tool, precise,
            so perfect in its hunt, we stand

stunned. The outcome: we witness the heron swallow
            dinner, swallow doubt.

Despite the earth's revolutions, I take home
            shallow steps, a self-reliance to ground

myself in a world slightly changed, a bit untarnished,
            continue in a realm benign.

Optic Neuritis

Everyone should experience it once.
To have the unwelcomed erasure

of 20/20 bliss, slowly have one eye blur
without shame, enough that trees become

flame. At night, instead of welcomed
darkness, lightning bolts against the ceiling.

What does one love to clearly see?
It's gone. Partially. Eyes have been

traded for moonstones. It's not genetic,
but the story emerges of an uncle

who stopped seeing after waving
to his daughter at the train station,

after receiving the news that bombs
had torn the old country to shreds.

Someone who knows more says
blame somatoform disorder.

But this ophthalmologist yawns.
No surgery to schedule, no meds.

A drive home that knows only
half the road. To wish this upon

the world may seem heartless, but
it's the same as wanting the earth

to be silenced one evening to hear
the cello pontificate. So much

is seen and heard that is not necessary.
So very much is heard and seen

that we could never live without.

I make love to my lesions

I say take my pleasure and give me back
my body.

I want it all back, not just the mind, but my beautiful

jaw before they drilled metal into the hinges,
before they taught me that the woman often

doesn't win. The word *submit* appears in the bible

and the implied meaning is up for debate.
Really, all I want is my body back. *My* body,

my not-really-Armenian-authentically, not-really-Middle-

Eastern-originally, not-really-American, which
means body-from-the-United-States body,

with a bit of Bay Area fog stuck in the curls, now straight lies,

body that learned to dance funk in Oakland
California, that unhinged body that circle-danced

to Fresno's zurna, duduk, dumbeg. Take me, sexy scars.

When you've tried everything else, and you can't
take the iron rods out safely because it's 30,000

bucks to properly extract, so you don't swallow mercury, amalgam

all the fancy words that means there is shit that they
called repair, to stop decay and made your father

poorer than he already was. Pathetic. Then this is what you do —

you make an amaretto sour, rum and Coke, brew.
This is assuming that the cause of the disease is dental work.

Clothes are off. It seems like a fair deal. No lesions

    on my brain and spine and you get to hold me.
    Grandmother's voice says a happy heart, the best medicine.

I've been laughing up a storm. Perhaps laughter is not happiness

    after all, but the machinery of the body undoing anger,
    readjusting bitterness and so the sounds that come out

are the mechanic's music. The guffaw. Brilliant. What a brilliant

    machine this body is. Except when intimacy reverses
    its roll. That summer we sanded the front bricks down

to get the ugly paint off, I thought if someone steps heavy on this,

    if someone just places a box down, these suckers will crack.
    Perhaps that's the lesion. The spot shaved down. The spot

weakened by wear. And then the weight. And then the breakage.

    We're going to try lingerie anyway. What is there to lose
    but more land for the unending, stubborn weeds.

Defining 50 Lesions

Father's sacred wrath made of carotid arteries
    shivering from Lebanon to Tamerlane

Drive, Mother's Syrian after-birth blood
    pressure over kitchen sink drains, cash

registers, returning thoughts that their mothers
    were buried under amber lights, died

quiet deaths, never mourned or chronicled,
    but felt like breaking old addictions,

could take its toll there in the hemispheres
    of brain matter and landscapes.

The science of neurology could coin
    a new name for all this fury.

Fifty seems large, a golden anniversary of some
    sort, a number the radiologist utters

as the final MRI results come in. Possibly a tally
    of losses, children who kept slipping away

moon after moon, while we sealed the cracks,
    walls of a fixer-upper that wouldn't mend.

Tally of surgeries, mouths of jerks, late nights
    to hospitals to check small pulses, wires,

(motherhood earns no doctorate degree), tally of no
    sleep, nights of caramel corn, coffee, reverse

neuroplasticity, the kitchen's metronome of noise. Fifty.
     Could have been a hundred. In dictionaries,

we move from entry words to origin. Psychological
     offense, five decades of consecrated debris,

snubs, silences turned into misinterpreted hieroglyphs,
     multiple scars of unlimited force and damage.

Partial Tubectomy Revisited

There are many reasons why a woman falls
to the floor. An optimist surely imagines
lovemaking, or the uncontrollable writhing

of modern dance that sweeps across the stage,
not a harsh plunge on hardwood, the tumble
so sudden one thinks the old furniture

has slipped, crashed, cracked the tile.
Let's work backward. She is lying there
screaming her husband's name. The right

tube gave up, gave out
like an old rubber tire does after much
wear. All it needed was a nail. All it took

was an embryo to get stuck along its path,
the pressure unbearable, and the day before
no increased human chorionic gonadotropin,

though twenty days of bleeding while
going back and forth to the hardware store
to mend the fixer-upper, same age as her,

fallen siding, withered eaves,
should have been the obvious sign.
So, she is lying there and the husband

rushes her to the emergency room
and she does not die as the doctor
said she would have had she not signed

the paperwork. When she wakes
she discovers the tube is gone,
couldn't be saved. On the television

an old black and white with wagons,
women in ankle-length skirts, poke
bonnets almost like a trap for hair,

boots full of dust, their hands rough
as pumice stone. And if these
settlers fell to the floor, she wonders,

who would come, who would hear them
and realize those long aprons had become
flags fluttering at the cabin door?

Harmonic Implications on Daylight Saving Time

Although we've sprung forward, lost one good hour,

we're all getting on with our lives.
This is what I'm thinking while the sky opens up

behind spring's dizzy birds, while Yusef Lateef's love
blows through the speakers, a charm that runs

further than the trek from Chattanooga to the Great Lakes,
wind vibrating off every bark and branch.

I love this world, too, despite all the people who have demands
on my time and all those daily chores that take naps

in piles around the house. I want my husband to tell me
I'm still his, sitting here against the open window's

bright calligraphy, near the beauty of insects,
who praise the mistakes of the creeping fig.

But I know he has to pay the bills first.
I don't want to resent anything anymore,

not the squirrels who won't let up and run all day
along the top cinder blocks of the yard, not the age

of my skin and all its implications, the power lines
interrupting the blue. I never knew an oboe

could make me cry, make me stop rattling dishes and draw
me to plum blossoms, to the clarity that comes when a man

decides to play a love theme. But I'm not thinking
of motion pictures or fables. I'm embracing all the things

I've learned these forty-two years—while the oaks
stood by—like how to play jazz in the ear of a butterfly,

how to catch Yusef's eastern pulse behind
his thick black-rimmed glasses, like my husband's

when we first met. I'm falling in love with everything
again, even the breeze that's become colder,

the house that's empty and ready to be fed.

Manifesto

After we make love, I think of the word *obliterate*

how it means the destruction of something. I think

hostile hands are everywhere. We should probably

nail it all shut. I don't have time to think back to

the fourteenth century because too much is tangling

roots this day and the day after. The sound of the word

obliterate is also beautiful, clean consonants, ping-pong.

When you love another, you really have to ruin a part

of yourself or each other. We could let go of the countries

we've proclaimed ours, come on, we live oceans, mountains

away. Modigliani's torsos stretched, the eyes without soul

yet riveting. There was a time I thought only a man

could say these things. The line repeats, refrain of my newfound

liberation: *after we make love I think of the word obliterate,*

how I want to ruin what's expected. Listen ageists, you can be fifty

and rule your own world. The real pandemic is in your heart.

Give me a stem-cell transplant for Christmas. I'm a wreck

sometimes. But I know how to spell phenomenology, and

I love some women who came before me. You kiss me

at every protest, while our fists unapologetically rise.

In Lieu of an Epilogue

When Your Mother Dies During a Pandemic

The walk down the hospital hallway
    does not frighten you despite

masks and gloves and gloves and masks.
    A woman wraps her purse

in a plastic bag, disinfects the soles
    of her shoes. Your mother. The last day

you will see this room. Since when did we blow
    air-kisses. Talk about a new norm.

Your mother is about to die. Weight of wires
    almost the weight of every world

she has known. They say maybe a malaria drug
    can save the world, could have saved

her dying father from an outbreak in Syria.
    The TV's volume is always

too high. There should be a specific word
    for the nerve it takes

to scribble *I want to leave this world*
    on a clipboard not meant

for one's last words. What is said and not said
    is poison no matter what. Don't love

what I say because you think you should. Love
    what you hear because it makes you

question everything. What was the point of
    calling something hopeful, a city.

What was the point in asking her questions
        when all she said was *I've done*

nothing—. No flashback can fix these moments.
        There's nothing sweet about loss.

You embrace no one. The measurement of six feet
        is your longitude and latitude and your mother

will soon be side-by-side with your dead father.
        You knew these were the last words to each other.

No one cried. The hallways full of masks and gloves
        and gloves and masks. You went

home only to hide. And the world is told
        to stay inside. Inside.

Pandemic Tally: At Odds with May

Apologies, mother, that you had no funeral. It was too close
to call the priest. Shovel of dirt. Flowers. Strangers with masks
in charge of lowering the coffin. Cyber condolences. Incense.

My sons face the screens. My sons face a future without most
of the people I loved. The teacher calls on those who are fast,
fed what they want for lunch. My sons clench their teeth.

All the funding has gone to the birds. Beautiful creatures, gleaming
feathers, whose babies have their feathers combed by aardvarks
and stool pigeons. These fledglings always get to bed on time.

Postpone the checkup, the procedure, the poetry of mourning,
there's a pandemonium of voices coming from a white tower
full of more fowl. Where are they all coming from?

Bombs. Children and mothers die together. They didn't get
a chance to contemplate as they did on school days. The forests
destroyed. Their husbands already buried. Conveyer belt methods.

I don't want to talk about kin, kinship or cognac. It always ends
with maps, my father's voice, my ancestors kneeling by graves.
I want everyone to stand up to choir it out. Even the dead.

There is no such thing as writer's block. There is no such thing
as writer's block. (Their favorite pencil was left in their usual café,
while the chandelier doesn't give its typical, shrewd light.)

Prison. In prison because they always wrote, even when they were
told that you are pissing off the guy in charge. The guy in charge,
when he was a boy they should have given him ripe apricots, pencils.

A reference to Donna Summer doesn't seem to fit the tapestry. Don't
see why not. Donna Summer lived in Los Angeles, she sang, ignited,
died. People still play her songs on the corner of Hollywood and Vine.

Dad, did you find Mom? Before she died she wanted to hear Elvis Presley
sing I Can't Help Falling in Love with You, but I don't know if that ever
was taken care of. She never told me if she missed you.

An antimicrobial resistant infection is not an easy thing to take care of
when almost everything is limited, when almost everyone seems
daunting with their masks and no masks and deranged attitudes.

I hear Grant Green's Sometimes I Feel Like a Motherless Child
while I wash another sink full of greens. Sometimes motherhood
is a well without bucket or rope. Even the blue sky still hunkers down.

Longevity: part pseudo-memoir, part commentary

My illness must be my masterpiece. No clever reference today. Things are different when someone's pressing your shirts. When I abandon myself, I abandon the word. Must mean my father spent most of his life deserting himself. Empty notebooks from Lebanon. My father did not take the right vitamins to save money. I'm sure of it. Changed his name tag from Vahan to Vaughn, for the same minimum wage. The wealthy debate on tea and how to redecorate. Sometimes I feel like being a conventional husband so I don't have to think about the order of meals and what they contain. Maybe if I just stay quiet, now that the children have stopped their joyous screaming, now that it's clear that no more money is coming in, now that each morning the ceiling is the same blank page bearing all names but yours. Fragment. Of course that was purposely a fragment. Show me one death that is a complete sentence. No syntax either. The dead have not returned in various forms or incarnations. Maybe this is how bitterness begins. The nerve of lemon blossoms, catkins to continue. Always the sky as the unshakable backdrop, always my mother who maybe could have survived had she let go of all from Aleppo. In and out of the mind. What else is there. Why I can't let her go yet may have much to do with—[Muriel, please don't think of me as a coward] people with newly painted shutters, crown molding, the ascots of the rooms, how they shine like the wives. Even the atriums have got attitudes. I'm sure outer space could supply even more answers. How to make it music, the bitterness. If I could become a woman again, you're damn right I would. [Godmothers, help me.] You see, there are floorboards in a woman. And this time I'd wear the tough boots longer. The doctor smiles, says eat more salmon. I say beans are cheaper than salmon. Maybe *you* can buy me some salmon. In a pandemic, you realize many things. For example, how much your hair wanted to gray. How marrying the right person is better than liquor and silicone. My father used to tell us don't be a dead fish, *tsoog*, floating down the stream. I wonder what type of fish he meant. The doctor, the wealthy are not the fish. They eat fish. They expect laborers to wear masks. Neither husband nor wife worry about the order of meals and what they contain. They don't offer salmon, but water. Their teeth are so white, like fishbone, bright as a supernova.

Flare-Up: Week Eleven, Twelve

To feel the ocean without
         the ocean.

I have come to the shore
         watching his arms

hold what is dearest and most
         dangerous

our sons bookend him while
         a seagull

ponders what I've chosen
         to eat.

What good is it if limbs don't
         know sand from stone?

In the moment I remember
         metaphors

of what we force onto each other
         even if we

mean well. This weakness, like
         the driftwood

wants to knock me over. Watch
         my refusal

cup the lips of my husband, who
         sees me

writing despite scribble, tremble
         wet paper,

the trash that incessantly comes in
          with the tide

is no accident. Pose the question
          to the injured

nerve, the crumpled mitochondria,
          to have innate

immunity, to let go of the crap
          they left me.

And who is they? The music sits
          in vibrato. Refrain.

Guess who they are and you are
          one step closer

to buoyancy, you've almost unlocked
          a rip current

almost used mortar, pestle, to grind
          the nearest

               shorebreak to bits.

Lexicon

Inspired by the painting Synchromy in Yellow *by Paul Sérusier*
Note: there is no commonly used word for motherhood *in Armenian*

There will be no words to impress them
for many years to come. All she will speak of

will be *apple* and *goodnight*. Maybe just monosyllabics
of her new life, their new life—*one, two, three*

and *see the dog run*. If she says there is a *synchromy*
not synchrony, of stars in their eyes, no one will be amazed.

If she says hieroglyphs are strewn in their hair,
no one will care at all. Although for years she studied

the cuneiform of her grandmother's veins,
although she wrote letters to the stolen orchards

of her childhood, the embossed chalice of the altar,
although she felt an alchemist in every thought

that blemished her mind, there will be no syntactical
charm good enough for the man who receives

the envelope in the mail. Silly morphemes, exaggerated
consonants, and the vowels, the vowels will suffer

like lost insects between rocks in a deluge.
So, why does she even try? Why, don't you know?

Once upon a time there was a word, and that word
was babbled with the restraint of a child, and it grew

into the magnanimous black uttering of a crow.

The Disease in Me May Be a Demigod After All

If you want to see my genius

to my father, who believed in

worth a bag of cracked wheat.

alive. God, don't let me also

Where's the lesser magic.

I can say it in a complete

Scars. Father. Root canals.

my eyes open from the

procedure? Wash the driveway.

bombing showers Beirut.

we aren't asked to do. Everyone

are entitled to a rank they never

settle, I could be bona fide.

I didn't think demigoddess.

surrounded by fan clubs full

No one went very far.

as hell. It's interesting. This

give me the money never given

serendipity. Ransacked spirit

I'm up all night keeping his habits

be afraid of my children.

Here. Finger to key, divinity.

sentence. Or I can do this, too.

His face proper and glad to see

procedure. Isn't everything a

Notify the local relatives today

We give ourselves jobs that

at some point believes they

earned. If only my head would

My quest, cure could rest in why

A man sat with maps. Others sat

of department stores mannequins.

Perhaps that's bitterness, mean

wasn't what I wanted to say.

Ability

Hard to understand why suddenly the phalanges
      metacarpal bones

give up for seconds every few minutes. The median,
      ulnar nerves

in argument with the thenar muscle group. Out
      of three, only one

gets to speak. Like siblings with one who thinks
      their complaint

is larger, grander deserving of sympathy, respect.
      Adductor pollicis

wants to move everything. I want to write,
      type, but the keys

smoke, fog under the fingertips while thoughts
      are too fast.

Work of the devil, grandmother would have said.
      Want to do good

and suddenly I've lost ability, one morning
      the day before

I had to tell the children, again, someone
      they love

has died. Acupuncturist, chiropractor, may even
      have to contact

the co-pay collectors, who lost their poster
      and its glory

proclaiming the Hippocratic oath. Being insulting
        to others is not

going to pave the body's patchwork back together.
        But sure feels

damn good. To give 'em hell, like the ninety-nine-
        year-old told me

was her secret to longevity. But who to
        give it to? Hell?

Are thumbs, siblings, muscles, nerves,
        doctors

all in the queue? A clue rests in the words
        of my mother

who never typed the story of her life.
        She should

have given them all hell before she took
        her last breath.

Unclaimed new pathways of brick, stone.
        She should have

left them stunned that her hospital
        bed was left all

made up as if finally she took off
        on her own.

My Shaking Hand Will Not Determine My Fate

While the coffee puddles on the floor,
        it is one key at a time. I don't wipe it up

yet. An idea clear as the coffee pot's glass body,
        and if the index finger on the right side

can hit *th*, *in*, a bit of a reach for *e* then anything
        is possible. I don't remember a thing about

training my infant hands to become masters of
        the toddler's kingdom. I don't recall

the struggle of the first snap, holding a pencil
        as if the entrance to Lorca's gate.

Granada was only one of many places we went.
        Afraid of the Spanish heat, afraid that

beautiful tiles and tapas would keep us there forever.
        Los Angeles can be just as hot, just as

charming. I just need something to let up. Calling
        on those gone to put in a good word for me.

I'm almost done with this sentence. Barely began
        what I was meant to do. Mention I need

a real lifetime. Tell whoever is in charge I have to move
        slow. I'm dreaming of pomegranates and train

rides. My lover's pants were pressed the day I knew.
        I have desire tough as titanium. Touch

of granite in my delivery. My hand moves with spark,
        with rage, against the inevitable page.

To have a backbone can also mean to have spunk

The doctor at the homeopathic medical practice
      has written "giddiness" under my diagnosis.

I think *I could have told her that* as well as *I'm not
      that giddy. Maybe after an amaretto sour.*

She mentions encouraging my body's homeostasis
      and I realize that I don't know

what that means. Maybe I've got to stop being
      giddy and get serious. Could be why

I'm so behind in almost everything. Then I look up
      giddiness. All the synonyms, all these

decades. I must have misunderstood so many
      well-meaning people. People I called

monsters or idiots may have been just using
      a word I did not know the meaning of.

Maybe when they said so-and-so's work was brilliant
      they just meant so bright you couldn't

bear reading it. Maybe when my old lover said you
      are overwhelming, he meant too much

like a good cup of cocoa. People need to be careful.
      Like the good specialist who said

my mother only had a thimble-sized space left
      in her lungs to breathe. I knew very

well that a thimble is not a slice of bread or bucket,
      no, a small cup that crowns the fingertip.

My mother used those to shorten the pants, dresses
        all our stupid clothes that kept coming

her way. What I mean by stupid could fill volumes.
        [Forgive me.] To make time for that would

be as silly as thinking a word could ever diagnose me.
        Immeasurable. Magnanimous. Broken.

Fixable. Apprehensive. Funky. Unfinished. Mis-
        diagnosed. Misbehaving. Always. Deal.

Jagadakeer: In Remission

1. History

My father said there were no other
words like the compound words
in the Armenian language.

For example, *jahgahdahkeer*, which means
fate, destiny. If you break the word
apart, *jahgahd* means forehead, *keer*

means letter, letter of the forehead,
or the writing on the forehead,
meaning fate, destiny may be allies.

There is something both beautiful
and terrifying at the thought of words
left there above the brows, below

the hairline, untamable, unpredictable.
If it appeared to us, would it say
divorce, dropout, theft, early death

or *seventy years of the same meaningless work,*
modern-day hermit, or worse, *mother of five who*
dreamed of the ballet every noon, heart attack?

Would his have said, *minister, misery,*
could have made it to ninety, if things
became cobblestone, cash, courage?

2. Exam

This is not a painting, chameleon,
manifesto or book. It is mine.

Even if thievery was attempted,
nothing would come to pass.

In the past, I left the antiques
by the curbside. Wrote a story

for the tanbark. Now the song
is encoded. Mine. Unrepeatable.

Exam: MRI Brain Without
and With Contrast

  History: Multiple sclerosis

Technique: Multiplanar and
multisequence MRI of the brain

was performed before and after
the IV administration of contrast.

Contrast: The patient was injected
with 12 cc Clariscan from a 15 cc

single-use vial with the remaining
contrast being discarded.

  Comparison: Brain MRI from August—

Findings: Numerous foci of—elongation
are noted predominantly in the periventricular

white matter with appearance characteristic
of multiple sclerosis plaques. The largest is in—

On the post-contrast images no enhancement
is seen in any of the foci to suggest

active inflammation. Normal gray-white
matter differentiation is preserved.

The cavernous sinuses are symmetric
and unremarkable. Ventricles.

> *no enhancement is seen in any of the foci to suggest active*
> *inflammation*

Compared to prior study, there has been
a significant interval

> *decrease*

in the number and the sizes of the foci
of signal abnormality consistent

> *with disease progress.*

Impression: On the post-contrast images
no enhancement is seen to suggest active inflammation.

> *Compared to prior study, there has been a significant decrease*
> *of signal abnormality consistent with disease progress.*

[end of diagnostic report]

3. Technique

Jagadakeer in Armenian
literally means forehead-letter
or perhaps the letters
the forehead illuminates.

My father would correct me,
the writing on the forehead.
To be the master of what's
coming, supernatural or not.

I hear my father say
the word *providence*,
speak of decrees of nature,
this is where his voice becomes

bass and tenor at once,
glorious vibrato for variation,
he declares that to embrace
the mysteries of the universe

you must be able to gaze
at hill and hummingbird
simultaneously. Panoramic.
Neptune and nest. Father,

at birth the word illness
must have been written
above my brows. Could it be
that the wrinkles now

are cross-outs? Where you
are now, do you see my rage,
sentences, printed or peerless
the test results strewn about?

Father, like my health,
could you cause reversal,
even if for a moment,
to stand at the front door

scent of coffee and pear,
eyes as amethyst, magnifying glass,
storm, brilliant igneous father,
wasted genius, brokenhearted

hidden man, come back,
pontificate. I'd like to show
you how things vanished.
I've written, unheard of, words.

Father, Baba, why do I try
to rebuild your story?
Can the body be rebuilt
if the story can do the same?

4. Comparison

Music can take me there. As can
my husband's midriff, larger

than the night I fake-punched it
at the World Stage. He tells me

Baraka is only the beginning
of what I have to read. Sonsonate

in his tremor, war his brass knuckles.
My father's camptocormia takes me there.

Mother's admission on her deathbed
takes me there. My father's love

of compound words in Armenian
takes me there. My mother's refusal

to dance takes me there. Yes, I'm
ping-ponging. My heroes are those

who love something from someone
they've never heard of. Nanig's

burning feet take me there. I don't
need help getting there. I just want

the White Bellbirds & roosters
to chill so someone can hear another call.

I will make sure my brethren haunt
you if you mimic me again. I will make

a projector reel playing your transgressions
in spiral form, a soundtrack, a gargling mess.

5. Findings

I get it now.
        Epigenetics is like the relative

who always shows up.
        The one who logs

what's incorrect with everyone else
        (Mr./Ms. unfinished-opus).

So, I may not need a stem cell transplant
        after all. Although saying

you just recently had a very successful
        autologous hematopoietic stem cell transplant

sounds impressive. Maybe even those who
        don't usually care will chime in.

You save yourself up to $50,000 in some cases.
        No, it's not poetic to have dollar signs

lead the sheep. It's not eloquent to have numbers
        rise above the conductor's rostrum.

Another set of MRIs and it feels like
        the tunnel's different this time around.

Decades later, a benediction for the body
        instead of the typical beratement.

I'm set on letting go with this. Set on
        disintegration, like absorbable sutures

that they didn't have in my parents' time.
        Another set of MRIs and this time

there's the ability to find one tune that matches
        the machine's buzz and racket.

Although it's a tunnel I can hear my family
        chattering, the kids complaining, hurry

back, even though we fight the longing
        for change. Set on reversing

what's exhausting. Like holding. That time
        the windstorm felt it could take

coat and hat, all of us at once, the hills a blur
        behind infuriated nature.

I'm set on being the first in the family
        to wear black with joy, I'm going

to marry myself first. There's no shame in
        vulnerability. I came face-to-face

with sorrow. This could be the beginning
        of not wanting what I was taught

to want. If the world won't ease up, I
        and my body will. If they won't shut

up, I and my body will shut down listening.
        Make it a vocation to allow miracles

in, in place of loser empires. I won't bring in
        the typical tropes. People get sick

of hearing of other people's losses. There
        it is again, sick. What if people got

quiet instead. The type of sound that repeats
        sleep-movements, sitting-breath,

forgiveness-overhaul. Like now, if I could
        just trust the tribulation's done.

This time the pictures will show a landslide
of healing, Morse code in the veins.

Get rid of your misery, the insect's shadow,
small in reality, large on the wall.

6. Impression

without contrast

The cavernous sinuses are
symmetric and unremarkable.

In medical terms the word
unremarkable seems to be

a good thing. No remarks
to be shaped or sculpted.

No marks with their weight
in cuneiform or comics.

However, when we say
remarkable, we know what

follows is stunning, memorable.
Perhaps my unremarkable days

need to be viewed as good. But
redefining is not that easy.

When I wake up, I want the day
to be over. I am not sure if this

is depression or not. Feed them:
breakfast, snack, lunch, snack, dinner.

Breakfast, snack, lunch, snack,
dinner. I know tomorrow and its

footprint will be the same. If
you want lyricism, find four

quarters, coin-operated vending
machines with toy capsules full

of trinkets galore. I curse the living.
I curse the dead. I know that I could

be building a fort made of paper inside
of me. I made a fort like that once

as a kid. No one was willing to help
me build a real one. Wood, log, flag.

All the rich kids had forts. I had
a lemon tree and no one looked

when I sat underneath it for eight
hours. Self-pity can be poetry. Try

it. Yes, you did and you were the
only one bravoed. I wonder

where everyone was. Eight hours,
I now realize, is a long time. I want

the day to end when I realize
that I woke up, orphaned,

a bit hungrier than yesterday. To be
this self-absorbed, to feel sorry for

oneself this much is a luxury. The
day should never be completely

over. Now I get it. This is a gift.
My fingers work today. I can hear

someone crying in the background.
I can get up. Even curse the breeze.

7. Impression

with contrast

Amor Fati. To remember the tin
shack, the tent. Embrace embers.
To love your fate seems a bit
like loving the wrong and right
of each morning, adoring pantheons
that don't bend, demons that don't
turn motifs from stone to saffron.
When you are a mother
the day reigns as a tyrant
the night a mental scourge.
Two uncles as poets. Syria the muse
of one, books the sulfur of pages.
The other, black ink, a long corridor
from 1975 strewn across balconies.
Talented men, men with notebooks
brass lamps lit at nightfall, always
broken. But what of the women,
the aunts? Was there not just one
who yearned for her voice beyond
the folksong, the hum above dishrag

wrung dry? If we go beyond *a widow*

embroidered. Threads to stabilize

a refugee's insomnia. Work toward

the morning, the school clothes,

the bazaar to raise money.

I went from Hygeia to Anahid

because I thought birth language

might be essential. The sounds

of Armenian, made of walnut,

apricot, cuneiform to monk.

My father held morphology,

syntax over a glass table,

telling me not to shatter

anything until I knew sounds.

Mother knew only syntax

of birth and bread, expected

nothing further except on

her deathbed. I can't find

a cure speaking an ancient

tongue that isn't mine. So,

I sing *sharagan*, folksong to

answer Anahid's open eyes.

She uses the dream terrain

to send this: *don't think*

the injured limb doesn't

grow its own alphabet,

ambition, to re-anoint

frankincense with loss.

If I find the connection of

how it is one body develops

lesions, the exact moment

of injury, can all be reversed?

Because really, coins left

on the trail sometimes works.

If I find a microfiche of the

newspaper that recounts

the exact time when my father's

family along with all the others

escaped Alexandretta to find

themselves in Beirut, Lebanon

1938 a nest of seashells, opening

of the New Port, can something

be remedied of my father's past?

If I rub limestone and chalk

between my fingers, create a fury

resembling my missing you

can I reach the top of the anticline

the mountains between you

and mother, before you met

can I clarify why we never became

what we set out to be?

ACKNOWLEDGMENTS

Gratitude to the editors of the following journals, publications in which these poems first appeared, some in earlier versions:

Adroit Journal: "Before the Elegy, Speak to Her" and "Pandemic Tally: At Odds with May"

Best American Poetry blog: "Sestina, as my mother cooks," appeared as part of the "Where My Dreaming and My Loving Live: Poetry & the Body" series

Boulevard: "The Tooth is Dead"

Gulf Coast: "Jagadakeer: In Remission—*History*," "Jagadakeer: In Remission—*Technique*," and "Jagadakeer: In Remission—*Impression with Contrast*"

Literary Matters: "Syllabics for My Mother"

Los Angeles Review: "Father dreams of Gibran," appeared in the *Los Angeles Review* online and was reprinted in the *Los Angeles Review* journal

Massachusetts Review: "Manifesto" and "Ode to Illness: rant in the form of monologue" appeared in "Revisiting WOMAN: An Issue, 50 Years Later"

Miramar: "Looking at the MRI Six Years Later"

MORIA: "Broccoli"

Nimrod International Journal: "If only he had written his refugee song," "Meditation on Fractured Vertebrae," "Ode to Their Leaving," and "Theorizing Vahan's Departure" won the 2022 Nimrod Literary Awards: The Pablo Neruda Prize for Poetry

Orion: "Needle Biopsy"

Pleiades: "Flare-Up: Week Eleven, Twelve"

Poetry Northwest: "The pharmaceutical that killed my mother"

Solo Novo: "Harmonic Implications on Daylight Saving Time"

Tin House: "Apology to the Body," "Optic Neuritis," and "Partial Tubectomy Revisited"

wildness: "Defining 50 Lesions"

Thank you to all the screeners, readers, and senior readers who believed in the voices of these poems, giving them a chance to move forward. Gratitude to the generous team at *Prairie Schooner* and the amazing staff at the University of Nebraska Press. With great humility I thank Hilda Raz, Ed Roberson, Kwame

Dawes, and Glenna Luschei for choosing this manuscript, for hearing these poems. A huge thanks also to Marilyn Hacker, Dorianne Laux, and Brian Turner. Thank you, Professor Dawes, for all the time spent on reading these pages, for your insights and guidance.

I thank the Money for Women/Barbara Deming Memorial Fund for their continued support of my work and the financial support given toward the completion of this book. Without their belief in my work, over the years, I would have been hesitant to continue believing the voices of my poems matter to others.

Thank you to the Academy of American Poets for including the poems "Apology to the Body" and "Partial Tubectomy Revisited," which subsequently appeared on *Poets.org*.

Many thanks to Camille Dungy, who chose "Lexicon" as a finalist in the AROHO Spring 2015 Orlando Prize Competition and who heard my poems, for her instrumental role in publishing several in various publications.

Immense gratitude to editor Eilis O'Neal, readers, and staff at Nimrod International Journal and Kaveh Bassiri for choosing my work for the 2022 Pablo Neruda Prize for Poetry.

Humble thanks to Mihaela Moscaliuc and Pádraig Ó Tuama for nudging my older work back into orbit.

Thank you to Lola Koundakjian, producer of the Armenian Poetry Project, for featuring some of the poems that appear in this book.

To those no longer in close proximity: Ms. Cheri from St. George's Preschool for major support, to Tim for delivering food to us when the pandemic took hold.

Personal note of immense gratitude to Dr. Jennifer Stevenson and Ms. Linda Evans for encouragement and support through pandemic, grief, and major surgery. To my new sister in poetry, Kate Sweeney. To Dorianne, for being my nerves, and Joe, for being Joe. To my friends, who like the stars, are brilliant and too numerous to name.

Remembering my father and mother, Vahan and Zevart Bedikian, and my father-in-law, suegro, Rolando Archila.

To my husband, the poet William Archila, the alpha and omega, whom I go to for honesty, to see if the poem sings. Boundless gratitude for our unaffected devotion and love while it all soars. There is no one else I would want to be stuck in a pandemic with.

To order or obtain more information on these or other
University of Nebraska Press titles, visit nebraskapress.unl.edu.